Copyright © 2022 by David Bot.

All rights reserved. No part of this publication may be reproduced, distributed or transmitted in any form or by any means, including photocopying, recording, or other electronic or mechanical methods, without the prior written permission of the publisher, except in the case of brief quotations embodied in critical reviews and certain other non-commercial uses permitted by copyright law. For permission requests, write to the publisher, addressed "Attention: Permissions Coordinator," at the address below.

Bot/New Harbor Press
1601 Mt. Rushmore Rd, Ste 3288
Rapid City, SD 57701
www.NewHarborPress.com

Ordering Information:
Quantity sales. Special discounts are available on quantity purchases by corporations, associations, and others. For details, contact the "Special Sales Department" at the address above.

Cataclysm / David Bot. -- 1st ed.
ISBN 978-1-63357-429-8

Contents

INTRODUCTION 1

I - God's Creation 3

II - God's Exhortation 7

III - God's Ethereal Instrument to Exist and Strive 11

IV - God's Array of One 17

V - God's Government: American History 23

VI - Pharisees and Tyrants: Humanity's History 31

VII - Hierarchy and Aristocracy: God's Colliding Arrays of Individuals 37

IX - Paternalistic Government 41

X - One Nation Under God: America Now 51

INTRODUCTION

Humanity is a deliberate creation. Each of us is a deliberate creation. And each of us is on a mission for and with God to survive, thrive, and create using God's gift of His ethereal spirit which He gives us each uniquely. Terrible, exciting, fearful choices await us alone but for God.

At the same time, we are part of a larger community that shapes us and for whom we have an obligation to try to help shape. But how in a sea of tyrannical inhumanity can we possibly avoid resignation born of despair and, thus, suffer defeat?

Focus on God, understand the context and enormity of the odds against each one of us, and choose carefully, courageously, and confidently. Now, strive . . . each of us . . . and together.

In the following pages, I offer my understanding of God's magnificent creations of the fine-tuned universe and all it contains. I also offer thought about our responsibilities to each other, as well as some of the problems we face today.

America is a cautionary tale of aristocracy. The founding aristocracy stepped into the pantheon of humanity's creation by demurring from the acquisition of power to themselves. Instead, they reserved it for God's individuals. This was in keeping with God endowing His individuals with life, liberty, and the pursuit of happiness.

I

God's Creation

The universe is all matter and energy, including the earth, the galaxies, and the contents of intergalactic space regarded as a whole. The *universe* is the realm where something exists and takes place. The *cosmos* is the universe regarded as an orderly, harmonious whole. *Cosmology* is the study of the physical universe considered as a totality of phenomena in time and space. Cosmology includes history, structure, and the constituent dynamics of the universe.

Dynamic is the word used to describe energy or objects in motion. Likewise, it connotes continuous change, activity, or progress. It is marked by intensity, vigor, and forcefulness. *Dynamism* is a theory or philosophical system that explains the universe in terms of force and energy. It is

CATACLYSM

GOD'S EXHORTATION, MAN'S SUBJUGATION

David Bot

New Harbor Press
RAPID CITY, SD

a process for the development of motion in the system.

God is the author of the generative, violent cataclysm that created the universe and its dynamic cosmos, a remarkable sublimation of a violent detonation of energy into harmonious creation. To *create* is to cause to exist and bring into being. The creation of dynamism was animated, invested, birthed through the violent production of energy channeled over time into a system that is harmonious and orderly; notwithstanding the change inherent in dynamism that continually threatens to end, kill, and extinguish the system, the dynamism, and the cosmos, should it become disharmonious, disorderly.

Why did God catalyze, create the cosmos? I think because God strives to create. He strives to create to find purpose to be. His purpose in creating humanity was that He might love . . . specifically, love us, humanity . . . and only perhaps be loved back as nothing is determined. He challenged and honored us by giving us free will. God was a catalyst as He precipitated the event and the process, the dynamism of creation, without being involved in the consequence.

God is at once majestically detached per our free will and intensely, coruscatingly, immanent because He is also inherent within us. God is the dynamism from which the cosmos was loosed. He loosed humanity as the quintessence of His creation of the cosmos. *Quintessence* is the pure, highly concentrated essence of a thing. His quintessence, humanity, is of Him.

Each individual of humanity is created with a soul. The *soul* is the animating, actuating, spiritual essence of an individual life. God created humanity in His image so, like God, we are to create. We have the opportunity to create in each moment and over time. Our soul, our mind, uses the raw materials of our senses, feelings, language, instincts, and reflective cerebration to synthesize creatively.

God created humanity in His image so that like God we are alone. Alone as individuals (ontogeny) and alone as a group of individuals (phylogeny). *Ontogeny* is the development of an individual organism from embryo to adult.[1]

---

1. *Metaphysics* is the branch of philosophy that addresses questions about the ultimate composition of reality. *Ontology* is the branch of metaphysics that deals with the nature of being. During the course of our ontogenetic development, our ontology is created as well. God examines us for our ontology. What we make of ourselves is our being. He examines us for our choices. He is patient, gracious, forgiving, and loving. Like His cosmos we are dynamic, and we can create.

Phylogeny is the evolutionary development and history of a species. However, unlike God, who is infinite and immortal, we are finite and mortal.

Like the cosmos, we violently, cataclysmically explode into life to begin the process of dying. We recapitulate the creation of the cosmos when egg and sperm collide. Energy is transduced, converted, transferred into the creation of life. Life is the quality that distinguishes a vital and functioning being from a nullity, nothingness, nonentity. Life is an organismic state characterized by capacity for metabolism, growth, reaction to stimuli, and reproduction.

But, our time of life is short. The context of our brief existence is that the cosmos is infinitely cold, empty, and hostile to our fragility, even while and even though God's love is in us; and, God loves us. It is bewildering paradox and sublime irony to contemplate the contrasts between the empyreal heavens of the cosmos and the living, fragile, feculent, fearful specks that are God's individuals, the whole point of His cosmos, His quintessence.

II

God's Exhortation

God's loving exhortation is perhaps, "I am with you and in you. Arise and strive" as He did to create us. Strive mightily and unceasingly . . . first, to survive to exist and then to exist to create so that we too might love and, thus, recapitulate His gift of creation and life. If we struggle, fight, reach, aspire, we recapitulate God's creative cataclysm of the cosmos and humanity, His quintessence. But, all the while that we are trying to apprehend God being in us and heed His exhortation to strive to live, His cosmos is indifferent to us. We are His quintessence and, simultaneously, our existence matters not to the cosmos. Death is not indifferent, however. Death stalks us.

The Greeks, Romans, Freud, and many others were students of life and death in God's cosmos. Eros from Greek mythology was the god of Love. He was the son of Aphrodite, the goddess of love and beauty. Eros represents creativity, sexual yearning, love, and desire. Eros represents sexual drive and libido. *Libido* is the energy associated with instinctual biological drive, including sexual desire. An *instinct* is an inborn pattern of behavior, a powerful motivation or impulse.

The death instinct is an innate, unconscious tendency toward self-destruction postulated in psychoanalytic theory to explain aggressive and destructive behavior. It is also called *Thanatos* from Greek mythology. *Thanatos* is the counterbalance to the Erosian life striving to the glory of God, the Creator. Freud postulated it coexisting with and opposing the life instinct.

God endowed humanity's individuals with both life and death instincts. There cannot be life without death for the purpose of definition as a necessary and delimiting, complementing contrast. Both are needed for the purpose of defining the other. Death and temporal evanescence inexorably bring urgency to the context of raging desperation in our striving to survive, create, and love in the roiling life-and-death struggle.

This is the context and the tension suggested by His admonition to strive.

III

God's Ethereal Instrument to Exist and Strive

Ether was a construct utilized in physics to describe an all-pervading, infinitely elastic, massless medium. *Narcissism* is God's gift and instrument of ethereal spirit, the philosopher's stone that transmutes our awareness, sentience of being alive with its attendant fear, exhilaration, despair into the striving necessary for surviving, flourishing, creating, loving.

In Greek mythology, Narcissus was a young man who pined away in love for his own image in a pool of water and was transformed into a *narcissus*, a flower, with a trumpet-shaped central crown (perhaps to shout out his paradox of agony and ecstasy).

Today, narcissism has a narrow and pejorative context of excessive self-love together with a lack of empathy for others. In psychoanalysis, it is the erotic, Erosian pleasure derived from the contemplation or admiration of one's own body or self, especially as a fixation on an infantile stage of development. However, narcissism most often is dynamic and sublimates. To *sublimate* is to modify the natural expression of an instinctual impulse in a socially acceptable manner. It connotes growth, progression, evolution, maturation. Thus, narcissism is not extinguished as we pass out of our infancy. It is sublimated. Narcissism is our sword, our Excalibur, wielded to strive to survive, prevail, and, hopefully, to excel throughout our lives.

So, for most, the infantile narcissistic stage is a temporary sojourn in the development of our ontological character. The individual's narcissistic awareness of his interaction with and contemplation of his environment requires a plastic, evolving dynamism to adapt, lest we perish in an importunate, impertinent cry of protest while being vanquished by Thanatos, our death instinct, in God's cosmos.

We strive to attempt to live, to flicker lambently, if only fugitively, in the cosmos. Our life is our opportunity for conversation with God to examine what kind of steward we have been with His gift of life. We speak to God with our life, and He will judge the account of our faith and creation to His glory.

Narcissistic sublimation in mythology is possibly Eros maturing into Apollo, the Greek and Roman god of sunlight, prophecy, music, and poetry. To be *Apollonian* is to be harmonious, measured, ordered (like the cosmos), and balanced in character. To be *Apollonian* is to manifest creation, growth, and improvement in one's ontological journey through life with God.

Contrast this evolving sublimation of narcissism with a devolving descent of narcissism from Eros to Dionysus (the Roman equivalent of Bacchus). Bacchus was the Roman god of wine. A *bacchanal*, or *bacchanalia*, is a drunken, riotous celebration or orgy. A *bacchant* is a boisterous, frenzied, orgiastic character. Literally, wine was the intoxicant of choice for Dionysus, but, metaphorically, power is the seductive intoxicant that writhes, twists, contorts narcissism's competitive drive in a dark direction that perverts, corrupts, debases our relationship with ourselves, other people, and God.

A malign perversion of Erosian narcissism to Dionysian devolution is when an individual of God successfully uses their narcissistic gift to attain successful accomplishment but then uses the power attendant to the accomplishment to harm other individuals of God by subjugating, enslaving, or even destroying them.

Narcissistic devolution to subjugating self or others is an expression of the Thanatos death instinct. Subjugation of one's brother, another of God's individuals, does not mirror how God treats His quintessence and, therefore, it is a false path for any individual of God to subjugate another person as well.

A healthy amount of narcissism is required by the individual to exist, flourish, and create while fending off the hostility, at worst, and indifference, at best, of the cosmos along with a competitive cohort of peers who are also God's individuals. A healthy narcissism is also required to countervail one's own insidious, pernicious, perfidious death instinct.

Generally, the narcissism of most individuals is, at least, relatively overwhelmed by the onslaught of these combined malevolent forces. In the end, we all go to God, but, undoubtedly, God is pleased if we utilize to the fullest the opportunity of life, He has given us and then render all glory to Him in our thanks.

Our narcissism is a manifestation of God's love for us. Narcissism is His ethereal gift of a weapon against temporal despair and death. Narcissism is God's ether that must be used with nimble alacrity to strive, reach, push using our inner striving restlessness of life as our polestar to travel with God. We should help each other to foster our respective narcissism.

However, if our narcissism that leads to accomplishment is used to acquire power harming, destroying, or subjugating others and, thus, rejecting God's example, we should forestall the ontological ruin of our soul by taking our hubris to God for salvation.

IV

God's Array of One

God's cosmos is ordered. The fundamental unit of God's cosmos is the number one representing each one of God's individuals. Every individual is alone . . . a flock of one . . . with God as our Creator and our Shepherd. But, for God, we come aborning into the world alone. But, for God, we exit life alone.

Existentialism is a philosophy that emphasizes the uniqueness and isolation of the individual in a universe that is hostile, indifferent, or both. It regards existence as unexplainable and stresses free choice and responsibility for one's actions.

This is a largely accurate, appealing, albeit frightening framework—except it leaves out God. With God our existence is explainable. The explanation is that we are to strive to survive, flourish, and create before we die. It is a curious pattern of humanity to repeatedly exclude God, as if life is not difficult enough already. But God is accustomed to being forgotten, alone, even shunned. In His immanence with us, God knows what it is to be His impertinent, importunate creation, humanity, who forgets Him ceaselessly and then must find Him again. We are alone but for God and we are never alone because of God. With God, our teleological purpose and existence is explainable.[2] Our purpose is to strive with God's ether of narcissism to pursue Erosian, then Apollonian, creation to honor God.

Paradox is a contradictory statement that nonetheless is true. For example, arguably humanity's greatest musical accomplishment, "Ode to Joy" in *Symphony No. 9*, was composed while Beethoven was deaf. Life is a paradox that exhibits inexplicable, contradictory aspects that become explicable only with the apprehension of God's immanence. A *paradox* is also often a statement contrary to received conventional opinion. Conventional, received opinion in our zeitgeist often marginalizes God. We shun our Creator. We shun our only companion for all seasons.

---

2. *Teleology* is the study of design and purpose in nature. We exist for a purpose.

Received opinion, dogma, convention, custom, tradition are ordinarily wonderful starting points in educational apprehension and acquisition of our history and context of existence. Recorded Western civilization provides humanity with unparalleled received opinion and convention to study, understand our paradox, our *irony* (the incongruity between the actual result of a sequence of events and the normal or expected result). We should imbue and steep ourselves and our children in the convention that is our history with all its creation and all its ugliness. With our informed, creative narcissism we can make further contribution, creation, innovation to convention, and progress for ourselves, humanity, and God. We can understand the ironic paradoxes of our relationship with ourselves, each other, and our relationship with God. We can be Apollonian.

But, even with understanding and even wielding the Excalibur of our narcissism, we cannot create a complete antidote to our loneliness. Narcissism sublimated can eventually take us closer to each other but, paradoxically, it will always be a restless wedge as well. God is ultimately our only companion for all seasons.

God's Array of One and the Conundrum of Community

We are alone with our free will but for God. We are surrounded by the indifferently hostile cosmos. We are also surrounded by our ostensible companions in humanity; except that where two or more people are brought together, even in God's name, hierarchies both beneficent and malignly subjugating ensue.

Humanity tries to imitate God's cosmos and bring order to its community. However, almost without exception, subjugation of one kind or another follows. Our ultimate antagonist is our own paradoxical ambivalence about ourselves but more about that ontological conflict anon. First, we address our penultimate antagonist, our brother, in preparation for confronting ourselves.

Ostensibly, the indifferent cosmos threat, as represented by the availability of food, shelter, and health care, is presently minimized by the advance of humanity's civilization as administered by and provided for by national governments and cultures. (This has been best accomplished by the free markets of capitalism.). But civilization is a thin veneer with little redundancy for the safety of God's individuals. The cosmos probes at humanity's gate indifferently but inexorably. Inside humanity's gate there is carnage among God's individuals going back to Cain slaying his brother Abel.

Thus, the greater immediate threat to the individual's life, striving, free will, and choice depends on the external threat of who is ruling the society, culture, or country, which, paradoxically, ironically, is ostensibly tasked with protecting us from the indifferent cosmos and from each other.

<u>v</u>

God's Government: American History

The only country in the world whose government was built to serve rather than rule God's individuals is America. The Founding Fathers built the country around individual liberty as a right bestowed by God. God served us by creating us and continues to serve with His immanent companionship. It is, thus, consistent that God's individuals would, in turn, desire to serve their country, America, as it was founded as a natural extension of God's design for His individuals to strive to create for themselves and, thus, serve God.

The Declaration of Independence veritably thunders, "We hold these truths to be self-evident, that all men are created equal, that they are endowed by their Creator with certain inalienable Rights, that among these are Life, Liberty and the pursuit of Happiness."

Likewise, the preamble of the American Constitution begins with "We the people " and crescendos in the phrase "blessings of liberty." In America, the individual is at liberty to strive to exist, live, and create as God intended. God is the Creator, not the president. The President is not a ruler, but rather a steward of the people, the individual citizens of God, so that they may serve themselves, their country, and God. The President has aegis to protect God's individuals from our enemies, our terrorist brothers, both foreign and domestic, while and so that they may strive for themselves to the glory of God.

The recognition of the primacy of the individual's freedom to strive and pursue his happiness through striving in his relationship with himself, God, and the rest of humanity illustrates that the Founding Fathers were moved by the hand of Immanent God. The cosmos was filled by the light of the evolution of man so that he might pursue his relationship with God and with himself unencumbered and undistracted. This primacy of God's individuals' right to liberty is *the* basis for American exceptionalism.

History records no other civilization, culture, country built around this primacy, this preeminence of the ruled as their own ruler, rather than another individual of God ruling them. In the history of humanity, it is an astonishing concept and accomplishment. It redounds with God's admonition to each individual to strive in keeping with God's array of one.

The neophyte founding American aristocracy hurled the liberty of the individual citizens aborning into history. They forbore the opportunity for the usual human inclination to avarice for personal power to metaphorically empower their countrymen with the same liberty God bequeaths all individuals. The raucous, caroming cast of Founding Fathers, at spiritual, intellectual, emotional liberty metaphorically mirrored God's gift to themselves, their countrymen, and posterity. George Washington declined to become an American King George. This accomplishment by the Founding Fathers of empowering the individuals of God was a paean of grandeur and glory to God. It was a political, governmental, social "Ode to Joy."

Peradventure, this could have been regarded as the end of history as the Founding Fathers had emulated God in the granting of life, liberty, and the pursuit of happiness to its citizens. What could go wrong? Surely, the world would become America!

Two hundred years later, there was discussion of the end of history when the totalitarian Soviet Union collapsed. Such conclusions about the end of history failed to apprehend the inherent tenacity of humanity's death instinct, which is a parallel companion to the individual's death instinct. We have a dark inherent penchant to pervert narcissistically healthy competition and aggression into dark, fell subjugation of one another in the course of our narcissistic living and striving.

So, this disinclination to power by the neophyte founding aristocracy was a careful intellectual choice per contra to the usual automatic instinctual emotional inclination of God's individuals to strive to compete, albeit acquisitively, selfishly grasping for the power to subjugate other individuals of God.

Sharing power in order to facilitate individual achievement of creation is an Apollonian sublimation of competitive narcissism that humanity has not ordinarily or often reached in its phylogenetic development. The usual course of human events is to follow a Dionysian devolution. It is often after an initial achievement that God's individuals lose their bearings with their polestar of God. Narcissism becomes hubris and God is shunned.

Concerning governance, humanity (God's individuals) historically has demonstrated an instinctual, emotional, impulsive, immature predilection. Apollo sublimates, creates, elevates. Dionysus[3] splits, projects, and, ultimately, subjugates and destroys.

The Founding Fathers declined power in order to share and create a more profound power. The ruling aristocracies of other nations did not want to share power (liberty) with the individuals of God (their citizenry) they subjugated. This was why there was never a rush to become *America* by any other country anywhere in the world. Rather, the rush to become *Americans* was by God's individuals seeking liberty while

---

3. To *split* is to divide for the purpose of creating contrast in a reductionistic, overly simplified manner, often, for the purpose of derogation of another person or group. Projection is the attribution of one's own ideas, feelings, or attitudes to another as a defense against having to confront oneself.

the world continued to be a sea of subjugation, save for the American island bastion.

However, America itself chafed caught between its espoused ideal of liberty and the reality of its lingering subjugation of the most literal kind, slavery. A singularly vicious civil war preserved the chance that perhaps man could continue the path to render glory to God by emulating Him. The war was only the initial essential step in the journey of liberation from subjugation, however.[4]

4. The specter and essence of slavery lingered. Black Americans were subjugated in the Reconstruction period after the Civil War by terror tactics such as lynching. Their voting rights were harassed. Their children were subjugated educationally by "separate but equal" segregation.
In recent decades, subjugation has persisted to manifest in public schools. They are chaotic, fearful, violent places that have drug and gang infestation. Safety and striving for excellence have not been demanded as priorities of the schools and government. Thus, subjugation has an ongoing breeding ground.
"Whites only" policies were litigated and then shamed out of existence, but, ironically, other policies promoting segregation have replaced them such that Black studies, Black only societies, Black student unions, and a Black national anthem proliferate. This is a recycling of racism masquerading as virtue signaling.
Enslaving and subjugating are endemic in humanity as a perversion of the normal, healthy narcissistic drive to compete. There are a plethora of manifestations of subjugation. Splitting Black Americans off to a special and permanent victim status is one more affront and abets a lingering

America's individuals, as represented by their government by and for the (individual) citizens, strived and eventually subjugation of women and other groups receded as well. However, for all of America's success at striving to emulate God's gift to the individual to live, strive, and create, we are as fiercely beset from without and within as ever. Instead of the American history of human subjugation receding, one could conclude that history is darkening as individual liberty, not subjugation, sinks and recedes in America and the world in a withering fusillade on American exceptionalism where the

---

presence of slavery.

Critical race theory (CRT) is a desperate ode to despair propagated to split and, thus, control Americans while the Declaration of Independence and Constitution are paeans of joy for America and humanity. The abolition of slavery and subsequent lawful iterations to fully enfranchise Black Americans annealed American exceptionalism where every individual of God rules himself.

America used the corrections of her mistakes to evolve in Apollonian fashion. CRT is a frenzied bacchanal of death preaching devolution to racism, tribalism, hate, splitting, and projection. Finally, it attempts to institutionalize ongoing racism as a permanent part of the American tableau.

It is as a laughable as it is dangerous. This is America, so this dangerous speech must be allowed. We should listen carefully to what the CRT delineates. CRT adherents may preach despair, hate, and racism to their children as is their right as God's individuals in America, but can you imagine loving parents doing such a thing?

purpose of government is to protect and serve individuals, not subjugate them. Why the frenzy to exterminate and extinguish America and its exceptionalism?

Because America works. Thus, it is a threat to many foreign governments who worry that not only will their citizens emigrate, but also those who stay will want change. It is also a threat to some Americans who desire the rule of an elite aristocracy and not the rule of the community of individuals as a whole.

America is an Apollonian achievement and experiment in progress. It tolerates Dionysian disruption and encourages self-improvement from the bacchanalian wreckage of power devolving to subjugation. This will further our Apollonian inclination and alloy our strength if the devolution to the bacchanal does not destroy us first.[5]

---

5. Lincoln's "with charity toward all and malice toward none" approach to post-Civil War Reconstruction and World War II's post-conflict Marshall Plan are examples of Apollonian achievement after war bacchanals of destruction and death.
Perhaps something of that sort should have been offered to Russia after the collapse of the Soviet Union rather than simply celebrating our totalitarian adversary's devolution to self-destruction, especially since the Soviet Union is coalescing once more after the invasion of Crimea and Ukraine.

VI

Pharisees and Tyrants: Humanity's History

In the New Testament of the Bible, a *pharisee* is a person of power professing piety in a sanctimoniously hypocritical manner. Jesus confronted them vigorously and passionately.

There are various forms of government from representational to totalitarian. A *totalitarian government* as the name implies has total control over the individual so that the individual is consumed with being obedient and doing the will of his ruling masters. He is obliged to deploy much of his narcissism to survive the tyrant instead of striving to create for himself. *Despotism* (tyranny) is a totalitarian government or political system in which the ruler (a despot or tyrant) wields absolute, oppressive, subjugating power. Adherence is mandatory. Retaliatory malign consequences are certain for disobedience. Thus, God's individuals ponder their alternatives of an arbitrary, immediate temporal death versus living a terror-filled life of subjugation.

On the other hand, representative governments cede a certain amount of freedom, autonomy, liberty to individual citizens albeit with limitations, regulations. These representative governments seek to find a balance between the power of the state to rule their citizens versus the liberties of the citizens to be free to rule themselves, but then, the state reserves the final, ultimate decision for itself. This is *paternalistic government*.

As a British statesman compellingly observed with concinnity, "power corrupts, and absolute power corrupts absolutely." This occurs in representative democracy as well as totalitarian government as elected representatives are vulnerable to an erosion of perspective as a function of time combined with the bacchanalian allure of power in the governmental hierarchy and aristocracy. Likewise, God's individuals in the judicial and executive branches are embroiled in the competitive jostling in the political hierarchy and aristocracy. Thus, it would be understandably easy or necessary for them to abandon their original and primary duty to facilitate the plebeian individuals of the citizenry to be at liberty to strive and create. To be stewards of the people could be inimical to their careers.

For most of history, most of humanity has been ruled not in the context of individual liberty but by tyrants of variegated stripes. This is a completely human perversion of what is the ultimate relationship which is the relationship between God and each individual human being. Ruling human aristocracies have always failed to discern this fundamental relationship to their ultimate detriment and demise in every single case.

The proper and limited role of government is to keep peace between men. It is to keep men safe and free from one another. It has become convention that the role of the individual human being is primarily about serving the powerful individual-turned-tyrant and his aristocratic entourages or the paternalistic democracy rather than himself and then God.

Communism is a type of totalitarian despotism, authoritarianism, absolutism. Communism stems from the word *commune*, or *community*, whose members share common interests, work, and income and often own property collectively. Communism began as a theoretical economic system characterized by collective ownership of property and the organization of labor for the common advantage of all members. Communism evolved from a theoretical economic system to a system of government in which the state controls the economy, and a single party holds power, claiming to work toward a social order in which all goods are equally shared.

Communism may have been something once seriously considered and well-intended, but its theory is completely bereft of an understanding of humanity's proclivities to compete and subjugate one another. There is nothing equal about God's individuals. We are all unique which lends itself to the evolutionary adaptation of the species. We compete and jostle one another in the process. We subjugate each other as a matter of course. It is the exception when we do not.

For example, individual liberty in China under the Communist Party is absent. The title of the Party is "Communist," but the communes are for God's individuals composing the general citizenry and the palaces are for the Chinese aristocracy. A fundamentally more accurate name would be the Chinese Totalitarian Aristocracy Party. It is thuggery threatening extinction, death to any individual espousing his God-given right to strive and create.

Totalitarian regimes are not about fastidious economic, social, or governmental constructs. They are about mercilessly aggrandizing power to the ruler or the ruling aristocracy of elites and eliminating the competitive striving among God's individuals to strive and create for themselves. It is all glory to the tyrant, not all glory to God.

God's cosmic array of one is composed of unique individuals in a singular relationship with God, not communes, communities, equals, groups, or nations. God's individuals are assailed and beset by any subjugation.[6]

---

6. *Populism* is a political philosophy supporting the rights and powers of the people in their struggles against an elite ruling class. *Elite* is a group or class of persons enjoying superior intellectual, social, or economic status.
The definition and meaning of *elite* is contextual as to whether it is meant literally or ironically. However, any elite class ensconced over time inevitably will rule in an increasingly tyrannical manner in keeping with human nature that competes and almost instinctually subjugates. Thus, even an elite steward of God's individuals should operate subject to term limits.

VII

Hierarchy and Aristocracy: God's Colliding Arrays of Individuals

Since an individual is unique, individuals are not equal. Because we are unique, we have attributes that come together uniquely. Individuals, like God's cosmos, are dynamic. We can and do change, but we always remain unique, distinct, and unequal.

What happens when individuals encounter one another? Whenever and wherever two or more people gather, we automatically arrange ourselves in such a way as to fill the vacuum of the moment and situation. Hierarchies are formed.

A *hierarchy* is a body of person's having authority. It is a categorization of a group of individuals according to ability or status. It is a series in which everyone is graded or ranked. Ironically, the term is even used to describe ranks of clergy and divisions of angels.

Humanity has hierarchies for everything as it is only efficient and practical. There are also hierarchies for those at the pinnacle of the ruling governmental and social orders. These hierarchies rule the rest of God's individuals in their respective nations and various groups ideally and ostensibly with the blessing and permission of the individuals being ruled; but, practically, this is rarely the case. Inevitably, corruption and perversion occurs and the rulers, being fallible individuals like all of God's individuals, almost inevitably over time lose sight of their relationship with God and begin to wield their gift of narcissism in a way that burdens and, eventually, subjugates their fellow individual human beings rather than serving them. This is a rule of humanity, not the exception.

The original individuals who become the authors, creators, of a governing hierarchy of a group or government are typically endowed some talent, penchant, or connection that has propelled them to the top of their hierarchy. Ironically, successful achievement may corrupt healthy narcissism because the successfully striving individual may begin to see himself as a god. Success in one area of striving does not usually equate with successful striving in another area, especially in the creation of stewards that protect and facilitate liberty for God's individuals to strive and create. More often, a tyrannical subjugator is the result.

Aristocracy is variously defined as government by the best individuals, or a small, privileged class, or by a small minority consisting of those believed to be the best qualified. *Aristocracy* is the aggregate of those believed to be superior or who believe themselves superior. They are the elite.

History records the course of humanity's aristocracies and how the function of time ultimately exposes aristocracy or transforms an aristocracy into a *kakistocracy* (government by the least suitable or competent citizens of a state). This temporal aspect of devolution and degeneration of aristocracy to kakistocracy is a mirror image of the individual losing his way in his relationship with God and using God's gift of competitive narcissism in a perfidious, corrupting fashion to create the evil of subjugation of self and his fellow individuals. The evil of subjugation is the suicide and homicide of aristocracies, empires, cultures, and individuals.

IX

Paternalistic Government

Pre-World War I royal monarchies were inept as stewards of their citizens, God's individuals. World War I killed millions. In the vacuum created by the failure and death of monarchial aristocracies, tyrannical despots took their place with their attendant retinue aristocracies. World War II ensued and killed millions more.

Despots in Germany and Italy were toppled and replaced by representative democracies similar to the rest of Europe that granted some individual liberty but also with constraints on the amount of liberty. These democracies are more paternalistic than America's. The European citizens of God elected representatives that had paternalistic inclinations. Their goal was not to maximize individual liberty for the individuals of God. Rather, their goal was to prevent more war.

The war-weary citizens did not trust themselves, so they created constitutions and elected representatives who did not trust them either. The citizens essentially elected strict, loving parents to parentally curb raucous, rebellious, martial aspirations of the citizenry while beneficently caring for the citizens. This is an eminently reasonable and understandable response considering what God's individuals in Europe had experienced. However, there are unintended consequences to ceding responsibility to even the most well-intentioned representatives.

God gave His individuals free will and, if those individuals are of a mind that they wish to pass on trusting themselves, they will certainly be able to find someone willing to accept the opportunity to parent/rule them. Thus, fledgling governmental aristocracies were created to foster pacific behavior while caring for the demotic populace.

The difficulty is that a paternalistic government does not recapitulate the phylogenetic development of the species or the ontogenetic development of the individual. Biological parents give way to children coming of age. A paternalistic government is permanent and becomes inevitably more paternalistic.[7] Individuals are effectively infantilized and confusingly ambivalent about the arrangement.

The culture resulting is dichotomous with an infantilized citizenry and a paternalistic ruling aristocracy. This is top-down rule setting up the same failed paradigm that has plagued humanity forever. God's individuals must take responsibility for ruling themselves from the bottom up as they prepare to offer their individual lives to God for examination. The capacity for determining who leads their country may not be within the grasp of God's individuals, but we need to try as it parallels, reflects, the individual's challenge to take responsibility for and rule himself. The responsibility for ruling themselves as God's individuals cannot be taken from them nor can they give it away, but their community of country can

---

7. In medicine, it is observed that an individual with dementia loses their frontal lobe governor which censors or sublimates the primitive outpourings of the rapacious primitive brain. Individuals revert to their unvarnished, instinctual expressions of their nature. They are still themselves, only more so. Thus, it is referred to as Moreso's disease. A paternalistic government inevitably suffers from Moreso's disease. It has no governor and becomes a caricature of itself.

be wrested from them, and generally is, as history shows us.

A paternalistic government does not remain fixed. A paternalistic government grows. Indeed, competitively driven individuals of God within the government seek to increase the scope of their competitive, narcissistic striving. They seek to enhance their power. One way to do this is to create more constituents for services provided by the paternalistic well-meaning government and the individuals composing it.

The striving individual citizen is effectively, relatively, discouraged while infantilization is relatively encouraged to further legitimize and enhance the paternalistically parental governmental bureaucracy. Thus, it operates the opposite of biological parents where fostering entitlement to dictate control of the offspring is not a desired or successful strategy.

Some individuals of God already have an innate, inherent reluctance and reservation to strive to survive and then strive to create. *Inertia* is the tendency of a body at rest to remain at rest. There is a resistance or disinclination to action. If a paternalistic well-meaning government offers a dependence-engendering alternative to striving, some individuals will eagerly take it because striving and life are daunting, frightening. Ultimately, if not enough individuals are supporting the system, the paternalistic government, and the entire corpulent system, collapses on itself.

Thus, a paternalistic government creates an unhealthy dependency, even its intentions might be well-intended by directing, dictating, requiring, and regulating. It usurps God's exhortation to his individuals to strive with the siren's song that there is an easy way through life and its fearful responsibilities.

For example, Europe has become Lotusland. In Homer's *Odyssey*, Odysseus, on his way home from the Trojan War, encounters a people subsisting on the lotus fruit causing the inhabitants to live in a state of dreamy indolence and self-indulgence. The individuals of God in Europe have been encouraged, enticed, channeled, obliged to strive less by their paternalistic governments, thus, countermanding God's exhortation to strive in life as individuals of God.

Instead, the state suggests that it strives for them. The secular god of the state has usurped, impacted, discouraged the narcissism of the individual to strive to create with the insipid, oblivion-inducing pabulum of the lotus fruit-cocktail to exist. This amounts to subjugation concealed in well-intended paternalism.

The state prefers a docile herd to jostling, fractious, unruly individuals striving narcissistically. A domesticated herd is more likely to be distracted with subjects like climate change. This ambiguous, nebulous topic moves at a glacial pace and comes complete with moving goalposts and fungible parameters to distract the citizenry from humanity's age-old nemesis of the subjugation that is man's inhumanity to man.

At the other extreme of paternalism's carrot-and-stick policy repertoire are curbing, constraining tactics. First, European speech is less free than in America. It is fussy, fastidious, intricately labyrinthine, byzantine, conditional, and, ultimately, brutally repressive as it endeavors to regulate the inevitable jostling occurring between God's individuals.[8] It betokens a tentativeness to trust the citizenry to embrace the responsibility of their freedom along with

---

8. Canada and Australia have especially strong heritage and tradition with Europe's United Kingdom. This includes the adoption of a paternalistic approach to governing. COVID-19 controversy has been leveraged by the paternalistic governments of those countries to brutally repress free speech while coercing compliance. Paternalism inevitably veers toward totalitarianism and away from individual liberty and self-rule.

governmental aristocracy's competing desire to wrest the power of the individual.

Second, taxes are higher in Europe. This constrains the liberty of the individuals being taxed. Incentive is diminished. The taxes are needed to pay for governmental largesse in benefits. A paternalistic government does not strive to create wealth, but rather the state strives to confiscate and redistribute what its citizens created while siphoning a prodigious portion of wealth to itself, such that the ruling aristocracy lives in dichotomous opulence compared to the citizenry. Anticompetitive corporate welfare and crony capitalism are other means by which subjugating paternalism pursues wealth rather than facilitating the pursuit of wealth by its citizens.

Almost universally visitors enjoy Europe. It is quaintly antiquated and docile. It is an anachronistic custodian of what it formerly was, both creatively and destructively, in its Apollonian and Dionysian history. Europe is attenuated.

Ironically, perhaps another layer of paternalistic bureaucracy is on the horizon in the form of a European Union government. All this paternalistic patronizing is on the shoulders of the citizenry, God's individuals, in Europe. However, the citizenry may have forgotten they are God's individuals and may think of themselves as the state's individuals or the state's children. The state would be God.

America, at least historically, has been ruled by God's individuals with the federal government as their ostensible steward, has been more technologically innovative, creative, and wealthier. America has provided robustly for Europe's defense while enduring European ambivalence as if the Europeans are uncertain about whether they are worth defending. In America, there is a dream of achieving onward, upward. In Europe, it is more circular than onward. The state cares for its children and the children support the paternalistic state without the expectation of ever becoming the parent.

Historically, Europe's Dionysian intoxicant of choice was power. Europe subjugated via colonialism. Europe in its shame, guilt, and self-loathing about war has now subjugated itself. God is honored by His individuals emulating Him. This is done by striving and creating. Neither the subjugation of others via colonialism and war nor the subjugation of self in shame, guilt, and capitulation are Apollonian and, thus, worthy of our relationship with God.

Curiously, Europe has not addressed the reality that other nations of the world are not dealing in the currency of the lotus fruit. Totalitarian regimes in China, Russia, and Iran still deal in the old Dionysian intoxicant currency of power. It is as if Europe is in a quandary as to whether to succumb by suicide of indolence or homicide of totalitarianism.

European representative democracy never trusted God's individuals with the full liberty God gave His individuals. They tried to produce a hybrid that has demonstrated itself to be staid, stolid, decaying, effete, enervated, moribund. The secular state has replaced God. The citizenry has chosen to yield their God-given natural rights to the state in order to have the state care for, control, and censor them.

The problem is that if the foundational citizenry limits their striving as individuals they may not survive. As individuals and as a culture, they will not survive the sterility born of indolence engendering corpulent paternalism. The idol of the state they have endowed with demigod status is not up to the task to do what they must do for themselves. God is in them, not the state. They must put their historical grief and guilt aside to strive once more.

X

One Nation Under God: America Now

America is a fascinating tale of two aristocracies. America's first aristocracy, as described above, stepped into the pantheon of Apollonian humanity with the ruling aristocracy demurring from the acquisition of power. Instead, they reserved the power to the individual citizens by giving them their God-given natural rights of liberty and responsibility without an intervening barrier of anything beyond a limited government to preserve safety and order among competitive men.

However, the death instinct of God's individuals and God's individuals as a nation stands athwart our arc of history. We must confront this in ourselves as surely as God is immanent in us. We are tasked and challenged by confronting the Dionysian bacchanal of devolution that we ourselves have wrought and allow to floridly luxuriate in our slide toward our own Lotusland.

In America, we have forgotten that we must strive not only as individuals but as a community of individuals. Because our rights are recorded in history and on paper, perhaps, we thought we were forever above the fray that ensnares the rest of humanity.

It turns out that we may not rest on the laurels of earlier generations' accomplishments. Rather, every generation of Americans must take its turn to re-earn our freedom and renew the vitality of the Founding Fathers' gift of facilitating God's gift of liberty to strive free of the tyranny of man. This unexpected struggle in America may thus be construed as a gift to strive for our place in the pantheon of man's creations to the glory of God.

We are discovering that the founding documents of America by their mere existence do not protect us from our brother who perverts the opportunity liberty provides to create, including creating subjugation. This is a manifestation of the death instinct.

The devolution of America's current ruling aristocracy is intoxicated by power while serving the rest of us with the lotus fruit of despair and indolence. A not-so-well-intended paternalism is spreading to America. When laws are ignored and set aside, when court decisions staying the lawless actions are likewise ignored, we degenerate into absolutism, despotism, and tyranny. How did this happen?

It has happened over time subtly, slowly, with our liberal speech devolving to illiberalism because our country necessarily allows for this in recognition of an individual of God's right to be at liberty to create the bacchanal of subjugation as well as Apollonian grandeur. Our vigilance to protect ourselves has not matched our tolerance of evil in our nation community of individuals. Perhaps, we thought someone else would sacrifice to protect us.

Do we engage in magical thinking because we have had a magical existence in history? We now anticipate a deus ex machina?

Who and what is the current American aristocracy? It begins with individuals. It begins with individuals who were given gifts by God. They wielded their narcissism with nimble alacrity to strive successfully and create immense wealth and power. They could have succeeded in their creation of wealth like this only in America. How rich the irony as they then turn from God and the country that has most successfully tried to emulate God's will of letting His individuals strive to create.

These elite men and women born of technological wealth creation joined an already established aristocratic hierarchal group, the American media. In never-ending irony, the public press, the Fourth Estate, which was once the champion of the individual American, dedicated to uncovering corruption and reporting truth, devolved to hating America, God's individuals that compose America, and finally God.

At the same time, God's individuals who compose the aristocracy of the media acquired an affinity, bent, penchant toward totalitarianism during a time when untold millions were killed and are being killed yet by totalitarianism. Additionally, generations of God's individuals in other countries have gone and continue to go without individual liberty for their entire lives due to totalitarianism. Americans perhaps became inured to the suffering of others in evil's grasp. Not surprisingly, evil has come calling for us.

The legacy media and the wealthy social media–technology aristocracy have united and turned from God and the individuals of the citizenry to lead the cabalistic takedown of American *exceptionalism*, which is God's individuals ruling themselves with the government being the elected stewards of the people not their rulers.

The legacy media, now in synergy with the wealthy entrepreneurs of technology and social media aristocracy, have the technical and financial means to direct and control America. They control communication. They control what gets heard and who does not get heard. They control the contextual narrative in which information is framed. They distort. This extralegal shadow government of the media and technocracy is so powerful because it intimidates and threatens with extinction any individual, or any other aristocracy, that stands before it.

This aristocracy of individuals turned from God when they turned their talents born of God's gift of narcissism from the original areas of their success in technology and communication to presumptuously believe they would be as successful in the arena of ruling other individuals. They hubristically believe they should rule God's individuals in America rather than the entire community of God's individuals ruling themselves through their elected representatives.

These brilliant individuals of God did not apprehend that America's rulers are not meant to be leaders, but rather stewards of God's individuals or, if they did know, they knowingly chose to flout God's will as the bedrock foundation of American exceptionalism. They presume to substitute their will for the will of the citizens, God's individuals. They must realize their ideas do not possess the merit to persuade, so they employ the artifice and subterfuge of media communication manipulation.

Their presumption to rule another man's life suggests that they have not learned the lessons of history. Their successful narcissism spawned hubris which, combined with their failure to appreciate the history of humanity, has left them not realizing that they are now the kindred of Stalin and Hitler. They have made the old error that men are to rule other men. God's array of one individual of God ruling himself in his relationship with God, in the context of a community of individuals ruling themselves through their elected stewards of the people, is the American experiment. Nothing else in history has worked as well.

The pharisees of technocracy and social media give agency to the lesser vassal aristocracies, to do their bidding, so that the media may stay cloaked above the roiling fray of debates that technocracy and social media contrives. Thus, any populist disputant has two opponents simultaneously in a debate. There is the ostensible antagonist opponent and the opponent-in-fact, the pharisaical media.

Any populist disputant should pay primary attention to the media tyrant to declaim their enslaving, subjugating. All other issues are of secondary importance if not fabricated, factitious straw men created by the media aristocracy to split God's individuals into warring factions rather than the respectfully raucous, but ultimately tolerant, community that we have the capacity to be.

Whether the subject matter is Marxism, communism, socialism, critical race theory, climate change, or viruses, the fundamental struggle is whether God's individuals in America will continue to be able to be at liberty to exist, to strive. Or, will the totalitarian, despotic, tyrannical rule by the unelected social media technocracy aristocracy subjugate the individuals of God?

The most striking evidence for this is the 2020 presidential election. The media technocracy aristocracy shadow government censored and demonized the incumbent despite his remarkable record of accomplishment. Simultaneously, they feted, coronated, the incumbent's challenger. The challenger had run unsuccessfully for president on three previous occasions, but at least he mounted a campaign.

In 2020, the challenger did not have the intellectual acumen to mount a campaign. He exhibited an emotional incontinence that went unchecked by any frontal lobe filtering or reservoir of reason.

The challenger did articulate awareness that he was intellectually compromised but, rather than withdrawing for the good of the country, he fed his still vast and vital hubris instead. His family knew he was compromised. His party knew he was compromised. The media technocracy aristocracy knew he was compromised.

This challenger had a long lineage of amoral expediency in public life. He always affected himself as a beamish shoulder-clapper, but this belied an elemental thuggishness. Altogether, he has conducted himself in his public life as a grotesque. But now, because of the ravages of time and illness, he is a senescent dotard as well. He is the social media technocracy aristocracy's pawn.

The media technocracy aristocracy shielded the challenger from the scrutiny that, historically, has been the role of the media to provide. The election outcome was an astonishing tour de force of Machiavellian malice perpetrated by the social media technocracy aristocracy. History will forever show that the social media technocracy aristocracy orchestrated the election of a literally feebleminded imbecile possessing twin deficits of truncated character development and dementing intellectual deterioration.

Other lesser vassal aristocracies to the wealthy social media technocracy aristocracy shadow government include much of academia, entertainment/sports, and business/corporate aristocracies. None of these wants to run afoul of powerful social media technocracy aristocracy wielding the capacity for narrative creation that could bring any other aristocracy or individual to its knees.

However, the most ironic, paradoxical vassal aristocracy contributing to the threat against God's individuals in America are many established Christian churches. For the ostensible representatives of God to be participating in the subjugation of God's individuals to the secular state that wants God out of America is astonishing.

There are exceptions. Some of the churches not willing to bend the knee[9] to the secular god of the wealthy media technocracy aristocracy tyrants are Evangelical churches. They pay the price of receiving wicked malign.

Perhaps an explanation for their bravery and courage is that the Evangelicals are often a raucous, fractious group in keeping with their fervor. Evangelicals are singled out for nefarious excoriation by a biased, agenda-driven, narrative-creating media technocracy aristocracy. For example, Evangelicals are routinely derided, maligned with poisonous accusations about the number of melanocytes they prefer in the skin's epidermis. Ironically, the media then focuses on rubescent necks and purported deficiencies in Neanderthaloid intellects. Evangelicals are ignorant racists is the message that the vicious, vitriolic media technocracy elite deliver. The media

---

9. *Evangelical* refers to a Christian church that founds its teaching on the Gospel (the four Gospel books of the New Testament). *Evangelism* believes in salvation through regeneration (spiritual or moral revival or rebirth) and in a transformed personal life marked by ardent enthusiasm.

desires to promote internecine carnage among God's individuals.

The social media technocracy aristocracy tyrants orchestrate this Balkanizing of groups of God's individuals in order to manipulate the chaos ensuing while staying concealed from the fray themselves. Few other religious groups are subjected to the obloquy that the Evangelicals are.

This is probably because of the Evangelical loyalty to the tenants of American culture which, in turn, are related to the Judeo-Christian foundation of America. These tenets are a threat to the totalitarian tyrants of the social media technocracy aristocracy. The media has declared war on religion if religion supports God and His individuals. They want a secular state that they control. They want a secularized church that they control. They do not want a country founded on God-given rights of liberty to God's individuals so that they may rule themselves.

In keeping with this, God's individuals in the Evangelical churches are among the most ardent voices in the literal life-and-death struggle over abortion. The Catholic Church was once a champion of the unborn, but when the Pope and the President spoke at their 2021 summit there was not a word about abortion.

It was illuminating, revealing. Abortion is the largest holocaust in history, but the Pope and the President spoke about the weather (climate change). It was similarly telling that when the current president's predecessor became the first American president to participate in the national right to life rally, the Pope was silent.

The Pope must live with his forsaking the unborn when the opportunity to speak to the world was before him. It may be inferred that the Pope is a purchased political pharisee of the ruling social media technocracy aristocracy.

The Founding Fathers built America on the foundation of God while barring His ostensible representative, the Christian Church, with the First Amendment's Establishment Clause. It was an ironic, paradoxically stunning discernment to keep God's individuals safe from the dynamics of humanity's hierarchies and aristocracies, including religious ones. God will not judge churches. He will judge His individuals composing them.

Why then did the Founding Fathers not discern and anticipate the watchdog for the citizenry, the Fourth Estate, the public media, abjuring and apostatizing their role and aligning with powerful men to subjugate God's individuals? Perhaps the Founding Fathers had limits to their perspicacity after all and they did all they could for us.

Peradventure, we are left with the gift of our own opportunity to strive to emulate the Founding Fathers to emulate God by saving American exceptionalism that government is to serve the individuals of God, so that they may create their own life with all glory to God.

Every generation has to be its own greatest generation and step up to the Apollonian task of renewing, creating, sacrificing, enduring against great odds. The present bacchanal of subjugating devolution is perhaps the greatest threat America has ever faced as all the aristocracies are aligned against God's individuals led by the wealthy social media technocracy aristocracy.[10]

The greatest threat makes for the greatest opportunity to strive, perhaps to sacrifice, and ultimately to create. Our American culture seeks to emulate God to His glory. We can construct our contribution to the creation of the American beacon to humanity.

FN

---

10. Elon Musk's purchase of Twitter may be a seminal moment in American and human history. It could provide the breach required to have a forum for uncensored free speech to illuminate the choice between Apollonian liberty versus Dionysian subjugation for God's individuals.

Ingram Content Group UK Ltd.
Milton Keynes UK
UKHW022005130423
420127UK00014B/1241